Magical PRESENTATIONS

A BLUEPRINT FOR MAKING EVERY **DIGITAL PRESENTATION** EFFECTIVE AND IMPACTFUL

RAJANIKANTH K

INDIA • SINGAPORE • MALAYSIA

Notion Press

No. 8, 3rd Cross Street,
CIT Colony, Mylapore,
Chennai, Tamil Nadu – 600 004

First Published by Notion Press 2021
Copyright © Rajanikanth K 2021
All Rights Reserved.

ISBN 978-1-63669-589-1

This book has been published with all efforts taken to make the material error-free after the consent of the author. However, the author and the publisher do not assume and hereby disclaim any liability to any party for any loss, damage, or disruption caused by errors or omissions, whether such errors or omissions result from negligence, accident, or any other cause.

While every effort has been made to avoid any mistake or omission, this publication is being sold on the condition and understanding that neither the author nor the publishers or printers would be liable in any manner to any person by reason of any mistake or omission in this publication or for any action taken or omitted to be taken or advice rendered or accepted on the basis of this work. For any defect in printing or binding the publishers will be liable only to replace the defective copy by another copy of this work then available.

Dedication

I would like to dedicate this book to my father, Late Shri Krishnamoorthy, who laid a strong foundation in building the inter-personal capabilities that moulded me into a confident individual.

Contents

Foreword 7
Acknowledgments 9
Introduction 11

Chapter 1: Magicians are the Greatest Presenters.
Great Presenters are Magicians .13
Chapter 2: Small Things. Big Difference. 15
Chapter 3: Five Magical Elements. 17
Chapter 4: Five Magical Elements: Briefing 19
Chapter 5: 5P's 23
Chapter 6: Great and Worst Presentations. 25
Chapter 7: How to Construct a Powerful Message 27
Chapter 8: The Magical Framework
(The Science Behind Magical Presentations) 31
Chapter 9: The TELL-Body 35
Chapter 10: The Power of Three. 39
Chapter 11: The TELL-Close 41
Chapter 12: How to Plan for Your Presentation in Just 5 Minutes . . .43
Chapter 13: How Not to Design a Slide 47

Chapter 14: Two Key Memory Techniques 51
Chapter 15: Paraverbal Communication 55
Chapter 16: Power of Pauses 57
Chapter 17: Mapping the Two Key Concepts .61
Chapter 18: Managing Presentation Nerves 63
Chapter 19: Engagement vs Participation 69
Chapter 20: Stage Walk 71
Chapter 21: Curse of Knowledge 75
Chapter 22: Audience Analysis Audit (AAA) .79
Chapter 23: Participation During Remote Presentations 81
Chapter 24: Hacking Any Tool for Online Presentations 85
Chapter 25: Sourcing Visual Images for Making a Beautiful Deck . . .87
Chapter 26: Handling Difficult Audiences Tactfully 89
Chapter 27: Making Numbers Meaningful 91
Chapter 28: The Outside-In vs Inside-Out Approach 93
Chapter 29: The Habit Quadrant 97
Chapter 30: Learning Everything is Not Important. Learning What is Relevant is Most Important 99
Chapter 31: The Last 'TELL' of the BOOK .101

About the Author *103*
References *105*

Foreword

Giving a talk/presentation in public is the second most scary thing for a person, the first one being – death! Almost a quarter of all people experience fear of public speaking, of dying on stage. If overcoming fear is the first step to making a presentation, making it engaging and impactful is the next big challenge. Most people may have a great story but are unfortunately poor storytellers. However, this is a skill that can be learned. I am delighted to see that Rajanikanth has broken down the entire process of making a magical presentation into simple doable steps – just five key elements.

The ability to communicate your ideas clearly and present them openly in a public forum is an essential component of success across several domains of life. Being a good public speaker can help you advance your career, grow your business, and form strong collaborations. It can help you promote ideas and move people to action on issues that directly affect them and also affect society at large. I have personally gone from being scared of public speaking to looking forward to doing it. From being scared of an audience to getting energized by it was a journey that took many years of effort. I have made presentations in front of thousands of people and in small board meetings – from hour-long sessions to 5-minute elevator pitches, every experience has been unique.

However, just as with any other skill, practice is the key to becoming a good speaker. Understanding the process and being able to follow a set pattern makes it easy to master the skill. There are simple tips and tricks here that you can use to make a confident, powerful presentation, whether it be digital, hybrid, or face-to-face. This is a book that I would have loved to have written myself, and hence when Rajanikanth asked me to write the foreword, I was honored and delighted at the same time. I believe this is a timely book that should be read by all professionals because one day or the other you'll be faced with the inevitable — having to make a presentation at short notice. In this book, you'll find a blueprint to guide you.

I am sure you will enjoy reading this book as much as I did. And I hope you will become a master at making every presentation magical!

V.R. Ferose
Senior Vice President, SAP Labs Silicon Valley
Founder, India Inclusion Foundation
31 December 2020

Acknowledgments

First and foremost, I thank my father-in-law, Shri. Kamalanathan (Ex-Station Director, AIR), for seeding the thought and motivating me to become an author. He is an author of more than 15 books on various topics.

Secondly, I thank my mother, Smt. Vijayalakshmi, for her love and blessings and for being a pillar of strength to our entire family.

Next, I thank my wife, Smt. Indumathi, for her unconditional love and support throughout my life. She is my best friend and a true companion.

Last but not the least, I thank my mentor, Shri. Ranganathan ('TransforMentor'), for being a lighthouse in each and every aspect of my life. His focused guidance has enabled me to reach where I am today.

Introduction

Thanks to the COVID-19 pandemic many impossible aspects of our life became possible. Presentations and meetings have moved completely away from face-to-face to a virtual mode. The new normal will be primarily digital and hybrid (digital + face-to-face) presentations. As classroom presenters, it is time for us to unlearn and re-learn key aspects since digital-style presentations are very different from face-to-face presentations. This book will transform you into becoming a confident presenter, capable of handling any digital or hybrid presentations.

Key differences between classroom and face-to-face presentations:

a. Participation is key in classroom presentations whereas engagement is the key in digital presentations. Engagement and participation are very different.

b. You can assess participants' moods through nonverbal cues in a classroom presentation. In digital presentations, this is not possible.

c. The setting of ground rules is possible in a classroom presentation. This is not possible in a digital presentation

d. You can demand attention in a classroom presentation, whereas you can only seek attention in a digital presentation

e. Group behavior of participants is very different from their individual behavior.

Chapter 1

Magicians are the Greatest Presenters. Great Presenters are Magicians

If you ask me the question: 'Who is one of the greatest presenters on earth?' I will definitely answer that it is a **magician**. Every time a magician is on the stage, magic happens. If you deconstruct any magic performance, you will see that the difference between a 'trick' and 'magic' lies in how a magician presents that trick. I became very curious about how a magician creates those magical moments and therefore started learning magic seriously. For the last three years, I have been learning magic skills by attending advanced courses and practicing those during my workshops and other events. Magic, so far, has been used primarily as a medium of entertainment, whereas, I started using magic as a very powerful educational tool.

While learning and researching magicians' styles of presentation, my research concluded that every magician follows **five key elements** to make a presentation magical.

Parallelly, for the second part of my research, I studied one of the greatest presenters in the corporate world, Steve Jobs, who made each of his presentations magical. On decoding several of Steve Jobs' presentations, I concluded that Steve Jobs also followed the **five key elements** to make his presentations magical.

Incidentally, a magician's five key elements and Steve Jobs' five key elements beautifully overlap with each other.

This book will help you understand what these five key elements are and how you can incorporate them in your forthcoming presentations, be they in Sales, Functional, Technical, Leadership or Management presentations. Let the magical journey begin…

How to derive maximum benefits from this book:

a. Keep one of your presentations (technical, functional, business, management, project), that you have already presented or one you will be presenting shortly, ready with you. This is a very important step.
b. At the end of a few chapters, there will be specific homework/exercises for each one of you to do. Don't ignore them. Do the homework/exercises before you go on to the new chapter.
c. Don't skip chapters. Each and every chapter is beautifully interlinked. You will be surprised to see all the links of the chain once you finish all the chapters.

Chapter 2

Small Things. Big Difference

Ram works in a software company and he is selected as a high performer in the telecom business. He gets a whopping bonus of one million dollars for his performance. Being a very intelligent person, he decides to invest his money. But Ram is confused about where to invest. Ram's father is a retired Chartered Accountant. He warns Ram that the market is volatile and insists that he invests in FDs (Fixed Deposits).

Ram does some research and finally shortlists two banks (FCI Bank and IBS Bank) based on two main criteria a) Credibility b) Maximum FD interest per annum. Ram will have to take a BIG decision selecting one of these two banks to invest a huge amount of money in. To validate his choice and take the right decision, Ram decides to visit both banks.

On a Tuesday morning, he first visits FCI bank. He informs the peon (office boy) that he wants to meet the Bank Manager. The peon requests him to wait at the visitor's desk and informs the Bank Manager. The Manager is very busy and he keeps Ram waiting for over an hour. Frustrated with the response time, Ram feels disrespected and leaves FCI bank.

The next day, Ram visits IBS Bank. He enters the bank and informs the peon that he wants to meet the Bank Manager. The young peon requests him to wait at the visitor's desk and informs the Manager. This Manager too is very busy and does not pay any attention to Ram. Ram waits for close to an hour and is frustrated, just as he was with the other bank. He decides to leave the

IBS Bank. When Ram is about to step out, the young peon comes running and apologizes to Ram for the inconvenience caused. He tells Ram that his Manager also conveys his apologies and promises to give Ram one complete hour, the very next day.

If you were Ram in the story, based on the above experiences, what is the BIG decision that you would take? Which bank would you invest a huge amount of money in and why?

If your answer is 'IBS Bank' and the reason for your decision is the behavior of the young peon, you are absolutely right. Ram took a BIG decision of investing a HUGE amount of money because of the small things that the peon did.

> *"When BIG things are the same, SMALL things make a BIG difference."*
>
> *– Ranga 'TransforMentor'*

Yes, friends, when BIG things are the same, SMALL things will make a BIG difference. Every great presenter focuses on the small things and that is why they become great presenters. If you take action on these small things, then the journey will turn magical. BIG things are similar for most of us, SMALL things are the differentiators. In the next chapters, you will be super excited to know about small things and the big impact that they can make.

Chapter 3

Five Magical Elements

I recently attended a very unusual magic show. The magician opened the presentation by saying that he was a digital magician and would perform the entire show only using three digital devices Mac, iPad and iPhone. This triggered lot of curiosity among the audience. He then called for an audience volunteer and asked him to inspect the stage. The person who was called to the stage was completely engaged in the show. Through this person, the rest of the audience seemed fully engaged too. Then, the magician narrated a personal story of his pet and showed a video of his pet using his iPad. To our surprise, the magician looked at his iPad and called out his pet's name. The audience was stunned to see the pet dog coming out of the iPad and running live on the stage. Finally, he closed with a powerful message saying, "Magic is a skill and any skill can be learned in just 20 hours." He referred to a book that changed his life called *The First 20 Hours* by Josh Kaufman. I want you to take a minute and think about what elements this magician used to make his presentation magical.

Let me take an example from one of Steve Jobs' presentations when MacBook Air was launched. Steve Jobs opened the presentation saying, "There is something in the air for you." He then brought different engaging visual elements to the presentation. Jobs told stories about the evolution of MacBook Air, Apple's association with Intel and their differences with Sony. With everyone in the audience agog for the first sight of the product, Jobs went to the table, picked up an envelope and gently opened it, pulling the MacBook Air out. He concluded that the MacBook Air is so light that it can even fit into an office envelope, leaving the audience thrilled and excited. This surprise element is one thing that people always remember even after so many years. Finally, Jobs closed his presentation saying that this was one of Apple's best products.

Now, I want you to take a minute and think about what elements Steve Jobs incorporated to make his presentation magical. In the above two examples, what were the common elements that the magician and Steve Jobs used to make their respective presentations magical?

The five elements that any great presenter uses to create magic are as follows:

a. Open with a high
b. Engage the audience
c. Tell a story
d. Have a surprise element
e. Close with a message

Please re-read the above examples to correlate the five magical elements. I am going to help you incorporate these five elements into your own presentations. In the next chapter, I am going to unpack the five magic elements in detail.

"It's still magic, even if you know how it's done."

– Terry Pratchett

Chapter 4

Five Magical Elements: Briefing

a. **Open with a high:** Opening a presentation is very critical to the success of the presentation. The initial 180 seconds will give a sense to the audience whether the presentation will add value, whether it will engage or be interesting to them.

Swami Vivekananda's opened his speech at the first World's Parliament of Religions saying "Sisters and Brothers of America… It fills my heart with joy unspeakable to rise in response to the warm and cordial welcome which you have given us." This opening sentence changed the way Americans perceived Indians. Many TED speakers start their talk with an incident or a personal experience to engage instantly with the audience. One of my CEO's opened his recent all-hands meeting with a statement mentioning the new growth opportunities available in a location unknown to many. This statement held the attention of employees until the end of the all-hands.

b. **Engage the audience:** You might have a great idea. But, if the audience is not engaged, the idea will fail to make an impact. There are different means of engaging audiences through face-to-face/remote presentations.

- **Smile**: A gentle smile, appropriate to the context of the presentation, will be a great value add. Smiles radiate energy through our voice tone during remote conversations.

- **Congruence**: 'What you say', 'How you say' and 'What they see' should be in sync at all times during presentations. If asynchronous, audience attention can wander. I have been to many presentations where what I see visually and what I hear from the presenter is completely out of sync.

- **Questions**: There are two types of questions 1) Open-ended questions, which trigger more details. Examples: What is your view on this? Why do you think this will work 2) Close-ended questions, which result in a binary answer (yes/no) Examples: How many of you know about this product? Do you agree with me? Great presenters decide the questions to ask much before the presentation. It is recommended to use more close-ended and less open-ended questions during short-duration presentations.

- **Pause**: A pause is a great engagement trigger that can be used during presentations. Pause is a temporary silence between two words. It is important to pause at key points/words to stress the importance of the point.

- **That's it**: I have seen many presenters ending the presentation with 'That's it'. The audience always remembers what is told last in a presentation. If you end the presentation with 'that's it', they remember only 'that's it'. Great presenters always end the presentation with the key message.

- **Humor**: Humor can create engagement in the presentation if used appropriately and timed well. Humor can be used only if it is practiced well. If you are not good at using humor, never try humor on the spot.

- **Voice Modulations**: Voice modulations are extremely critical to engage the audience. Especially in today's world when most presentations are virtual, it becomes extremely important to practice modulation before the presentation. Frequent pauses, stress on the words and varying the tone are the elements that will decide the impact of the presentation.

c. **Tell a story:** Storytelling is a very important skill of a great presenter. Whether it is technical, functional, business or management, the art and science of storytelling becomes extremely crucial. 'Tell a story' includes user stories (in an agile world), real-life experiences, personal stories, etc. Every technical/functional requirement originates from a user story.

d. **Surprise elements:** The definition of surprise element is simply 'what next'? People should not be able to anticipate what next. Magicians include many surprise elements in their presentations. Similarly, all great presenters use this technique very well. A technical expert who was presenting in a tech conference on security features of cloud architecture, opened the presentation with the picture of Paris Hilton holding a pet and giving an interview. Paris Whitney Hilton is an American media personality, businesswoman, socialite, model, singer, actress, fashion designer and DJ. He said that Paris Hilton lost millions of dollars from her bank account after this interview and this had to do with cloud architecture. Saying so, the presenter proceeded with his architecture, demonstration, algorithm and flow diagram. Curious to know how Paris Hilton had lost millions of dollars from her bank account, the audience lapped up every word. Before the conclusion, the presenter brought in the same picture of Paris Hilton and closed the loop.

The story goes like this. The interviewer had asked Paris Hilton a final question: "Ma'am, you are holding a beautiful pet in your hands. Could you please share your pet's name?" Paris Hilton revealed her pet's name. Hackers who were listening to the interview went to Paris Hilton's bank account and hacked her bank account by using the 'Forgot password' option. The most common reset password question is "What's your pet's name?"

This example shows the creativity of a presenter in introducing surprise element contextually in the presentation. Each one of us is creative and, with a little effort, we can easily incorporate surprise elements into our presentations as well.

"If you look for problems, you will find more problems. If you look for possibilities, you will find more possibilities."

– Anonymous

e. **Close with a message:** Every presentation has to be closed with a message. This is what people will remember and is called the 'recency effect'. Like opening, closing is another important factor that will determine the success of the presentation. Take time to close. Never be in a hurry. This is your last chance to leave an impact.

Chapter 5

5P's

Can you guess what the 5 P's of presentation are? Keep guessing...

Let me share my personal story. I was working for a German multinational company named SAP for a long time. Being a technical and product engineer, I had great expertise on a specific automotive product on both, functional and technical aspects. I can also communicate quite well. Whenever we had a client/delegate visiting us, my management team would ask me to deliver a presentation on the product I was working on. Every time I delivered such a presentation, I would fail miserably despite being an expert on the product and a good communicator. Do you know why? Think about this. Many of us think that if we are an expert on a topic, we can present well. Please mark my words: *You being an expert on a topic does not guarantee that you become a great presenter. You being a good communicator alone cannot make you a great presenter too*. The only aspect that can make you a great presenter is the 5P's: 'Prior Planning Prevents Poor Performance'.

The reason for my failure was that I was presenting all that I knew and not presenting what the client/delegate wanted to hear. This is a classic error that many of us make. As experts, we try to communicate all that we know and we think that will add value. There is a big gap between what we know as a presenter and what the audience wants from the presentation. Presentation is not about delivering what you want. Presentation is all about delivering what the audience wants. This can be only achieved with preparation. I have delivered more than 200 workshops on this topic called 'Magical Presentations' for a wide variety of audiences ranging from Senior Directors, Engineers, Business Experts, Brand Managers, People Managers and Product Managers. I found that if I don't prepare and practice for a workshop, the workshop will not create an impact and I have tested this quite a number of times. If I prepare and practice, I have seen real transformation happening during my workshops. Even though I know the content well having conducted more than two hundred workshops, I still prepare and practice for every one of them. Preparation and practice are two important pillars for creating magic in presentations.

> *"I am the most spontaneous speaker in the world because every word, every gesture, and every retort has been carefully rehearsed."*
>
> *– George Bernard Shaw*

A very interesting quote and it is an oxymoron. What do you think this quote means? It talks about spontaneity and it talks about preparation too. Yes, friends, this quote teaches us a very important lesson that there are no spontaneous speakers in the world. Every speaker who is spontaneous on stage has prepared so well that they appear to be spontaneous. Of course, Steve Jobs looks very spontaneous on stage, but he too has done multiple rehearsals for every presentation. A magician looks spontaneous too. Do you think a magician could pull off a show without preparation and practice? The only qualification of a great presenter is preparation and practice.

Chapter 6

Great and Worst Presentations

Can you think of one of the greatest presentations of your life? Take a minute. Mentally visualize the presentation. You could have attended such a presentation in your recent board meeting, technical seminar, sales presentation, remote presentation or a lecture during your college days. Write down in the space provided below why that presentation qualifies as the greatest you have attended. Now, think of one of the worst presentations you have attended. Write down in the space provided below why you classify those presentations as the best or the worst.

Great presentation: Presenter: _____ Topic: _____

Example: Engagement was high. Good use of humor.

a.
b.
c.

Worst Presentation: Presenter: _____ Topic: _____

Example: The presenter was reading from the slide. No audience connect.

a.
b.
c.

There is a specific reason why I am asking you to do this exercise. One reason is to know what qualifies as a great and the worst presentation. The other reason is even more significant. It is a fact that people remember only two types of presentations, the great ones and the worst ones. Unfortunately, people don't remember good or average presentations. This means, if we want our presentation to be remembered, we must make it either the greatest or the worst.

To deliver a great presentation, it is important for us to first have clarity on the definition of a great presentation. Steve Jobs is a great presenter. The current Prime Minister of India, Shri Narendra Modi, is a great presenter. Our past President, Dr. APJ Abdul Kalam, was a great presenter too. They all are great presenters although their style of presentations is entirely different. The qualifying factor is that each of them is able to deliver their message. If a presenter is able to deliver the message to the audience with clarity and impact, then they qualify to be great presenters. Each one of you can become great presenters with your own style. The only focus required is to deliver the key message. The good news is that I am going to give you a beautiful framework for delivering your messages powerfully to the audience. I have taken many of my students on this magical journey of becoming a great presenter. All they did was diligently follow the framework.

Chapter 7

How to Construct a Powerful Message

I am now going to unfold the framework starting with this chapter. This framework has been tried and tested across multiple categories of presenters. This framework can create magic for each one of you. So, fasten your seat belts and pay attention.

To construct a message, there is a three-step simple, yet very powerful technique.

TELL (Open) – Tell them what you are going to tell. How does your favorite hourly news show start on television? For the first few minutes, they talk about the headlines alone.

TELL (Body) – Tell the details. The news host goes into the details of every section.

TELL (Close) – Tell what you have already told. Please always remember what is told last is retained.

I was invited to speak to a group of Customer Service Managers and their target was to increase their Sales and Customer base. I am sharing the presentation script below. Please read the script closely. The script will reveal the framework. Please read this script visualizing that you are a Customer Service Manager.

My Talk:

Dear friends, I am going to share with you a technique, which can give you at least a 30% increase in your sales within a quarter and has the potential to double your customer base within a year. Would you be interested in understanding this technique? The name of the technique is called irresistible offer. I have taught this technique to many Fortune 500 organizations and every organization that has implemented this technique has doubled its Sales and Customer base.

I want to share some experiences with you.

a. Last year on Children's Day, I experienced a very interesting incident. Children's Day is celebrated across India to increase awareness of the rights, care and education of children. It is celebrated on 14 November every year as a tribute to India's First Prime Minister, Jawaharlal Nehru. There is a fine dining restaurant close to my home called 'Chutney Chang'. It's a pretty decent restaurant, quite expensive, serving good food. This restaurant, last Children's Day, printed a small pamphlet and gave it to every child in and around the schools in my locality. My son who was in grade eight also received the pamphlet. Looking at the pamphlet, my son was so thrilled and excited. He came running home, breathless and looking for me. He handed over the pamphlet to me and when I read it, I was super shocked. The pamphlet had the following message: "Dear child, on account of Children's Day, our restaurant would like to invite every one of you to have dinner free of cost. Don't miss this opportunity." My son, who was very excited, politely requested me to take him to the restaurant that day and I was unable to say 'No'.

When my son and I were discussing the plan, my wife, Indu, overheard our conversation. She came to me and gently asked me whether she could also join us for dinner. Having been married for more than a decade, I have clearly understood that whenever my wife makes a request, it is not a request, but an order. Incidentally, at that time my in-laws were also staying with us for a short vacation. After a few minutes, Indu again came to me and requested that we also take her parents along with us and again, I was unable to say 'No'. That evening, all my family members went happily to the fine dining restaurant and enjoyed a gala dinner – all, except me, who had tears in my mind at the thought of paying for all of us. My son's was the only meal that was free of cost. Was this not an irresistible offer given by this restaurant to attract more customers?

b. A few years back, one of India's top online retail giant 'Flipkart' (now under Walmart) launched an irresistible offer of purchasing USB's for one rupee ($.013 approx.). My friends and I wanted to take up this offer as it was truly irresistible. We started browsing the website and stayed on it for close to two hours. When we logged off, we were surprised to see that each of us had purchased many other products apart from the USB as the irresistible sale offer was only for five minutes. The whole strategy of Flipkart for launching the offer was to make users visit their portal knowing that they would be tempted into many purchases. Is this not an irresistible offer given by Flipkart to attract more customers?

c. I want to share a third example. In 2006, I was traveling to Germany by Lufthansa. When I reached the airport, there was an announcement that the last 10 passengers from their list would have to take the next day's flight to Germany. Unfortunately, that list had my name on it. I was shocked. I already had a confirmed ticket and had scheduled appointments with key stakeholders the next day. I went to the help desk and asked them the reason for bumping us off the flight. The lady in charge answered that the flight was overbooked.

Flight overbooking is normal practice in the airline industry which I was unaware of then. Ticketing agents book a greater number of tickets than the available number of seats to minimize losses from cancellation. On some days, everyone turns up and the airline will then request the last 10 passengers to travel the next day. Seeing me frustrated, a gentleman who was Lufthansa's Customer Service Manager offered to help. He told me that he would give me two options. The first was the option of traveling the same day for which he would request for an exchange with some other fellow passengers.

The second option that he suggested was truly irresistible. The offer was that if I did agree to travel the next day, then the airlines will pay me Rs. 35,000 in hand ($465 approx.), arrange accommodation at Leela Palace (the only seven-star hotel in Bangalore) and arrange a BMW for pick up and drop. I turned to the Customer Service Manager and said, "When are we going to Leela Palace?" Was this not an irresistible offer given by Lufthansa to retain their customers?

Dear Friends, an 'Irresistible Offer' is not about giving more money but giving more value to the customers. By practicing this technique and using this appropriately, you will be able to double your revenue and increase your customer base. Now, I want each one of you to take 10 seconds and think about that one irresistible offer you can make to your customers.

Thank you, friends, for the opportunity.

My talk ends here.

Chapter 8

The Magical Framework
(The Science Behind Magical Presentations)

I am going to unfold the magical framework starting from this chapter. For you to understand this better and grasp the concept fully, I request you to read Chapter 7 once again. A couple of questions before we deep dive into the topic: If you were a customer service representative, has the presentation impacted you? Did you think the script was engaging and beneficial? Surprisingly, each and every step of my presentation was crafted based on the magical framework. All that I followed was the 'TELL-TELL-TELL' framework. Let us analyze the elements under the first TELL. Let us discuss in detail the elements of this framework.

TELL (Open): My opening had three important segments:

a. **Explaining how it benefits the audience:** "I am going to share with you a technique which can give you at least a 30% increase in your sales within a quarter and has the potential to double your customer base within a year." Every person who is attending your presentation is only interested in one aspect. This aspect is called 'WIIFM' – 'What Is In It For Me'. The audience is only interested in knowing how they will benefit from the presentation. If a presenter is able to communicate clearly the benefits to the audience, then the presentation will open with a high. This is also called 'WIIFT', which means 'What Is In It For Them'. Do you have experience of attending all-hands meetings or Town Halls? Most of the all-hands or Town Halls fail in the opening because the presenter is unable to articulate what is in it for the audience clearly.

b. **Overview of the key message:** "The name of the technique is called irresistible offer." It is important for the presenter to give an overview of the key message at the start of the presentation. The audience should have clarity on the key message during the start of the presentation.

c. **Build credibility:** "I have taught this technique to many Fortune 500 organizations and every organization that has implemented this technique has doubled its sales and customer base." Building credibility is very critical to the success of the presentation. The audience should know why they should listen to you.

d. There are three P's to build credibility with the audience.

   i. **P-Person:** Build credibility for the person. During every one of my presentations, I make a conscious attempt to talk about my achievements, expertise on the topics and my research on the subject. It is important to do this to gain trust from the audience since credibility is directly proportional to trust-building.

      i. I have five patents in my name on this machine learning topic
      ii. I come from a strong technical background
      iii. I have researched this topic for the last five years

   ii. **P-Process:** Build credibility for the process. If your message is related to a process, then it is important to build credibility for the process.

      i. The agile process has been globally accepted by Fortune 500 companies and has huge benefits of meeting customer expectations early

ii. The feedback process that we are implementing has been globally researched, tried and tested across geographies within our organization

　　　iii. The productivity of the entire business unit has increased by close to 40% after the process was followed by every employee

　iii. **P-Product:** Build credibility for the product or service that you want to sell.

　　　i. This fintech product will revolutionize the industry. It has received huge funding from one of the global institutions

　　　ii. This product was developed by leading experts in the industry

　　　iii. No other product can offer this flexibility as it was developed inhouse

To summarize, the first TELL (open) should have:

- Give the benefits to the audience
- Overview of the key message
- Build Credibility using the 3 P's

In the next chapter, we will talk about the second TELL in detail.

Chapter 9

The TELL-Body

I request you to read the TELL – Body section of Chapter 7 again. How many examples did I give as a presenter? What were the examples? What was the key message in each example? Please take 30 seconds to think about it.

Yes, you are right. The key message that I wanted to deliver was 'Irresistible Offer'. To deliver this key message, I gave three examples. The first example of Children's Day pointed towards the 'Irresistible Offer' message. The second example of Flipkart's USB offer also pointed to the 'Irresistible Offer' message. The third message on Lufthansa airlines pointed to the 'Irresistible Offer' message. All three examples highlight the same message and hence the message cannot be missed. All the examples were carefully chosen to resonate with the audience. The examples will change based on the audience. Even if one among the audience misses the connect through an example, the other two examples will make sure that the key message is not missed. The number 'three' is a magical number derived out of a lot of patterns from science that it makes a deeper impact on individuals. Depending on the time available, more examples can be used. The TELL-Body can contain examples, experiences, personal stories or facts supporting the key message.

I am sure some of you reading this chapter will have a question on whether there is a possibility to include three examples for any kind of presentations. The answer is 'yes' and it is possible using the F-B-E-A quadrant. Using this quadrant, you will be able to easily bring three examples.

The powerful F-B-E-A quadrant:

FACTS What do you want people to **Know Factually?**	**BELIEFS** What do you want people to **Believe Intellectually?**
ACTIONS What do you want people to **Do Actively?**	**EMOTIONS** What do you want people to **Feel Emotionally?**

FACTS: Some of your audience will take decisions only if they are convinced by the facts that you provide supporting your key message. Facts involve evidence that can be proven and data that cannot be debated. Examples of facts are: a) Company revenue for the previous year; the thickness of a laptop measured in inches; the productivity hours logged for the last month. The presenter will have to research and gather facts in order to deliver the key message.

BELIEFS: Some of your audience will take decisions only if you make them believe intellectually that your idea is the best. Examples of beliefs are: a) The economist believed that the whole world will enter into a recession because of the COVID 19 (Corona Virus Pandemic) and there were no facts supporting it at that point in time. b) Most times, the stock market trends of going up and down are based on the belief that investors will react in a specific manner because of news that would have occurred the previous evening c) In our research center, we have to make the management team believe that our prototype should be productized to increase profits d) An architect convinces the engineering team to move to a new platform by showing them the benefits of the tool where code optimization and code reusability is efficient.

EMOTIONS: Another set of your audience will be convinced to take favorable decisions only if you can trigger emotions through your examples. Emotions have the power to make a deep connect and hence can be powerfully used in your presentations. Examples of emotions could be: a) Insurance agents use the knack of selling a policy by triggering emotions on life's safety and security b) The stock market becomes bullish or bearish based on the investor's emotions of fear and greed c) The operations team getting a buy-in from the leadership for approval of new headcount by triggering fear of possible attrition in the team due to work overload

ACTIONS: If you can bring an example by fact-belief-emotions, then the audience will take the action that you will want them to take. In the launch presentation of MacBook Air, Steve Jobs gave many examples (Facts-Beliefs-Emotions) with the intent of convincing the audience to take action: that is, buy the MacBook Air. Interestingly, he never directly makes a statement that you should buy one. Actions can be explicit or implicit based on the context.

There is no definite order to the F-B-E-A framework. Examples of Facts, Beliefs and Emotions can come in any order. Be creative in bringing examples/stories into your presentation. A great presenter is the one who can tell powerful stories.

Chapter 10

The Power of Three

Whenever we want to start something, we say '1,2,3… start!'. Three is more than just a number. It holds a profound religious, cultural and philosophical significance. Scientifically, three is the optimum number of choices that a human brain can process at once. Beyond three, our brain will expend more time and energy. Three is also the least number of elements required to create a pattern. Hence, this combination of pattern and brevity of choice results in more memorable and compelling content.

Research gives further evidence on why three is the magic number. One recent study found that in advertisements, speeches and other messages designed to have a persuasive effect, three claims will persuade, but four or more will trigger skepticism – and may even reverse an initial positive impression.

Three options make it easier for you to order without having second thoughts. Yet another example where the rule of three plays a trivial role, will be the number of choices given to you while purchasing a car. If you pay close attention, your dealer will offer you three segments to choose from – Subcompact, Compact or Family, and Luxury. Once you have chosen your preferred segment, you will be given three choices – Hatchback, Sedan or SUV. For each of these variants, the dealer will show you three of their best cars. This will prompt you into making a purchase.

The rule of three is also avidly practiced by keynote speakers and influencers. For instance, Steve Jobs used three adjectives: "thinner, lighter and faster" as the headline for the 2011 iPad 2 launch. In his 30-minute-long speech, it was these three adjectives that people noticed the most. In fact, the entire internet was writing articles on the iPad with these three adjectives as the title. Therefore, it is safe to assume that these three adjectives did influence people to buy iPad 2.

US President Barack Obama is a great example. Not only was his campaign slogan "Yes We Can" composed of three words, but his speeches are peppered with groups of three.

To create such a powerful and compelling speech, you should first choose three identical or three different words for your headline – just like Steve Jobs did. Once you have chosen a headline, the next thing that you should do is to write three messages that support your headline. An important point to note is that both headline and messages should relate to the overall theme of your product, service or thought. Following the choice of the three messages, the next step is to have a set of three supporting points for each of your messages. The last and final step is the application. If it is a product, idea or a message that you want to convey, give three examples or points. The supporting points can be statistics, examples or anecdotes. Apply this framework to convey a powerful message to your audience.

Chapter 11

The TELL-Close

The closing of a presentation is very critical. This is what you want the audience to remember after they leave. It is your final chance to make an impact. Don't miss this opportunity. During my closing (refer to Chapter 7), I ensured that the three segments were covered.

a. **Reinforce the key message:** "Dear Friends, Irresistible Offer is not about giving more money, but giving more value to the customers." It is important to remind the audience of the key message and reinforcement becomes a key factor. The presenter will have to explicitly reinforce the key message.

b. **Reinforce the benefits to the audience:** "By practicing this technique and using this appropriately, you will be able to double your revenue and increase the customer base." The audience is only interested in what they will get from the presentation. By this time, there is a chance that they would have forgotten the benefits. Hence, it is important to reinforce the benefits to the audience.

c. **Call to action:** "Now, I want each one of you to take 10 seconds and think about that one irresistible offer you will give your customer." It is the responsibility of a presenter to guide the audience on what they expect from them after the presentation through a call-to-action statement. Even where the message is clear the next action steps must be explicitly stated.

For instance:

　　i. I request you to let me know if we can go ahead with implementing this process for our team by next week.
　　ii. Can you please test this product and share your feedback by March-end this year?
　　iii. Can you please tell us how much budget we can expect this year for hiring new team members for this location?

To summarize, the first TELL (close) should have:

- Reinforce the benefits once again to the audience
- Reinforce the key message
- Have a call to action (for action-oriented presentations)

Chapter 12

How to Plan for Your Presentation in Just 5 Minutes

There will be many situations where you are given little time to prepare for your presentation. I have been in many situations where my Director would give me hardly an hour to prepare for the presentation. The technique that I am sharing with you will become so handy that you can prepare for any presentation in less than 10 minutes. This technique is called 'Mind Map'.

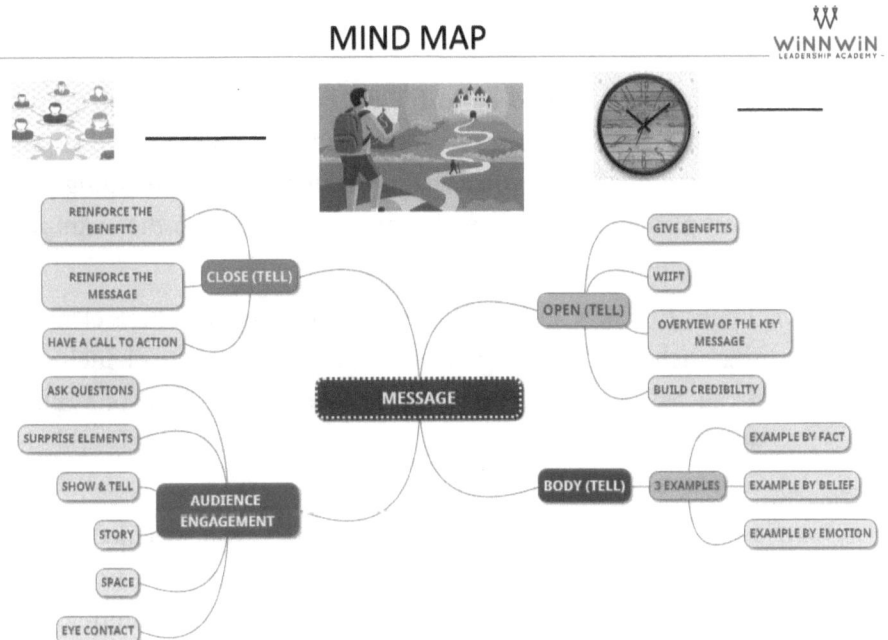

A **mind map** is a diagram used to visually organize information. A mind map is hierarchical and shows relationships among pieces of the whole. It is often created around a single concept, drawn as an image in the center of a blank page, to which associated representations of ideas such as images, words and parts of words are added. Major ideas are connected directly to the central concept, and other ideas branch out from those major ideas. *Source: Wikipedia*

Steps:

i. At the center of the mind map is 'the mind'. Similarly, at the center of the presentation is the key message. Take a sheet of paper and draw a box (circle, rectangle, etc.) around as shown. Write down your key message in the box.

ii. On the top left corner, write down who will be the audience for the presentation. In the top right corner, write the allocated time for the presentation. These are extremely critical and the message will change based on the time and the audience for the presentation

iii. Once this is done, draw another box which is the OPEN (TELL). The OPEN (TELL) has three elements. As a presenter, please fill in all the three elements.

iv. The next step would be to fill the BODY(TELL). This section will contain three or more examples based on the audience and the time. We have learned that the framework for providing three examples is the F-B-E-A. I request you to write the examples/stories in the appropriate boxes.

v. Then, fill the CLOSE (TELL). This again has three elements that include reinforcing the message, reinforcing the benefit and a call to action. You can decide to have more than one call to action based on the message and the audience. Please fill this section as well.

vi. Last, but not least. A great presenter will decide on the engagement techniques that they want to use even before the presentation. Hence, I request you to choose the techniques that you want to use for each of your presentations. For example, you can choose to use a demo and humor for the first presentation and stories and visual aids for the second presentation. Great presenters will even decide the set of questions that they will ask during the presentation. Use this engagement box to choose your own engagement techniques.

If you can master this mind map technique of preparing for presentations, you will start making a huge impact. Average presenters, first prepare the PowerPoint and then work on their messages. Great presenters first prepare the mind map focused on their message and only then add the necessary visual support through PowerPoint presentation. If you start following the second approach, the number of slides in your PowerPoint presentation will be much less and this is important to make an impact.

> *"If you do the same thing again and again, you will get the same result. If you want different results, you have to start doing things differently."*
>
> *– Albert Einstein*

Three important steps for making your presentation magical:

a. Prepare the presentation as though you would do it without a PowerPoint. Use the mind map.
b. Focus on the message and delivery.
c. Finally, use the PowerPoint to add visuals and key messages.

Chapter 13

How Not to Design a Slide

Communication effectiveness can be broadly classified into three parts.

a. **Verbal Communication:** The words that we talk
b. **Nonverbal Communication:** The posture, gestures, body language that we see
c. **Vocal Communication:** The tone modulation, pitch, volume of our voice

According to Albert Mehrabian the three elements account for our liking the person who puts forward a message concerning their feelings: words account for 7%, tone of voice accounts for 38%, and body language accounts for 55% of the liking.

Albert Mehrabian was born in 1939 to an Armenian family living in Iran and is Professor Emeritus of Psychology at the University of California, Los Angeles.[1] Although he originally trained as an engineer,[1] he is best known for his publications on the relative importance of verbal and nonverbal messages.

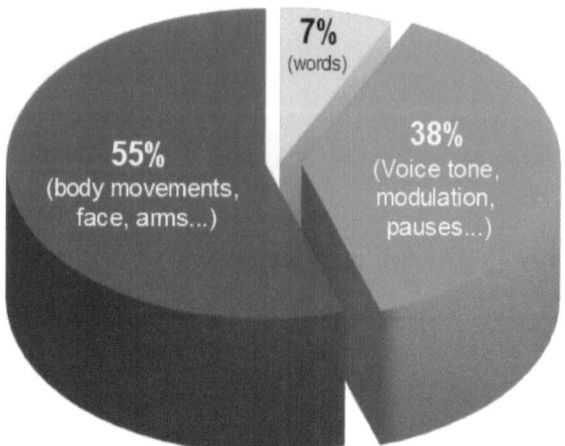

The study reveals that all three elements should be combined in such proportions to make the communication effective. Words alone will be less effective, as seen from the research.

If we apply the same logic to our slides, then verbal will denote the words, the nonverbal will denote the visuals or pictures and the vocal or paraverbal will denote the highlights that we use. In this section, I am going to give you the 10 golden rules for presentation. If you just follow these, you will be surprised to see your slides becoming fewer in number, yet highly effective.

Ten golden rules to designing your slide deck:

a. Your slides should be 70% visual and 30% textual
b. Have only neutral colors in the slide. This is important because you might have an audience in your presentation who are color blind and they might not be able to see certain colors. In addition, the projector can throw up a different combination of colors. It is safer to stick to neutral tones in the slides. Neutral colors are black, white, gray, and sometimes brown and beige. They are also called 'earth tones'. Use different colors only for highlighting.
c. It is recommended to have only one message per slide. I have seen presenters condensing multiple messages onto one slide which is definitely not presentable.

d. It is also recommended not to have more than three to five central messages in the presentation. The audience will find it difficult to remember more than five messages.

e. The use of appropriate animation is critical to a presentation. Please recollect the congruence in presentations that we discussed in the earlier chapters. What they see, what they hear should be congruent. Use basic animation to maintain congruence in presentations.

f. No long sentences in the slides. Participants will start reading a presentation instead of listening to you. As a presenter, it is important to take control of the situation.

g. Highlighting key messages and important data will determine the tone of the presentation. Use bold fonts, frames, colors to vary the tone of your slides.

h. Use font size > 26 in the slides. This will give a better visual impression and at the same time accommodate less text. Guy Kawasaki, former chief evangelist of Apple talks about his favorite '10/20/30' Rule of PowerPoint. '10' slides for '20' minutes with '30' as the font size.

i. Use Cut, Cut, Cut. Take every slide and ask yourself as a presenter whether you can cut the slide, cut the slide, cut the slide (three times). Even after this, if you are really convinced that this is an important slide, then retain it. This small exercise will help you retain only the most important slides.

j. Never use more than two font types in the presentation. Font types are like your handwriting. Keep them consistent.

Chapter 14

Two Key Memory Techniques

Have you been in a situation where you suddenly blank out either at the start of the presentation or anytime during the middle? Yes, I am sure many of you would have undergone such challenging moments during a presentation. Here are two techniques that have helped me greatly in remembering my key points:

a. **Linking words through a storytelling technique:** Let's do a small exercise. I am going to share with you 10 words and I want you to remember the words in the same order without looking at them again. Let's play the game in full spirit. The words are tree, hole, snake, well, frog, typewriter, milk, skateboard, airplane, James Bond. Now without looking at the words again, can you recollect the words in their order?

There is a very powerful technique that I have learned from a memory specialist called Harry Lorayne, author of the book: *How to develop a superpower memory.* Human minds cannot differentiate between what is real and imaginary. If I ask you not to think about five pink elephants, you will end up thinking about five pink elephants. Using this as a strength, Harry Lorayne talks about connecting uncommon words through a powerful imaginary story. The mind can remember stories more easily than just words and hence presenters can use this technique to practice linking uncommon words or messages used in their presentations.

Let me share an imaginary story connecting all the words. Please visualize the story narration. I want you to imagine a huge green **tree**. Within the tree, there is a small hole. From the hole, a poisonous **snake** pops out. The snake looks down and sees a deep well. From the deep **well**, a frog jumps out onto a typewriter and starts typing a letter. The paper that comes out of the typewriter is **milk**-white in color. Suddenly, the paper, milk in color, changes into a **skateboard** and the skateboard begins traveling at a speed of 100 kmph. The skateboard magically starts flying in the air and becomes an **airplane**. The pilot driving the **airplane** is **James Bond**. Read and visualize the story again. Now, in your mind, I want you to recollect the words loudly visualizing the story. Please try this technique a couple of times. I have used this technique a number of times during presentations and have benefited from it a lot.

b. **Index card technique:** Remembering numbers and key data points can be a nightmare for presenters. You cannot have all the information on slides or there could be a situation where you don't want to or are not allowed to use the slides. In any case, index cards are a useful backup tool. Index cards are palm-size cards that fit into your palm. It is an etiquette for presenters to carry index cards to their presentations.

If you lose your chain of thought or want to validate the right information to be given to the audience or go blank in the middle of the presentation, index cards can bail you out. Great presenters carry them all the time because they are very particular that they don't miss out on valuable information. Believe me, referring to index cards only increases the credibility of the presenter. TED speakers and C-suite employees are proud to use index cards in their presentations.

There are more uses to index cards besides memory aids. I use index cards to sequence my messages in the order of importance. Every index card will represent one key point or one message. When

I am delivering presentations, I will have all the sequenced index cards in my hand. Once the message or key point is communicated, I change the sequence of the index cards. At any point in time, the index card that I am holding on the top will represent the most important point which is very handy during my presentations.

Chapter 15

Paraverbal Communication

Paraverbal communication plays a very important role during presentations. The role of paraverbal has become more and more critical in today's virtual environment. It refers to the volume, pitch, variance of voice, pauses and stress on keywords.

Let us do an exercise: Stress on the underlined word

Vocal Stress Exercise

- **He's** giving this money to John... means that he gives money and no one else gives money to John
- He's **giving** this money to John... means that he is not lending money to John
- He's giving **this** money to John... means that he is giving money this money only to John
- He's giving this **money** to John... means he is giving this physical cash and not a cheque
- He's giving this money to **John**... means he is giving this money only to John and no one else

The person on the other side of the remote conversation will understand the significance of the word based on how you modulate during the presentation. Great presenters rehearse the script underlining keywords so that they know where to stress and pause during the presentation. Many presenters resort to fillers during presentations. What is a filler you may ask? A filler is what we use to fill the sentence when we don't get the next word. When we don't get the next word, we will fill that space with 'aaah, mmm, right, okay' and many other expressions. A presenter might not notice this unless they see their own recorded presentations. But the audience will notice this a lot. Hence, a presenter should develop the skill of not using too many fillers, as it makes them sound hesitant and uncertain.

Two techniques to overcome fillers are:

a. **Voice recorder:** A mobile voice recorder can be used as a powerful tool. I record my voice before any presentation and listen to my speech. I note what went well and where I can improve. This exercise also gives me an insight into the pace of my presentation. This could be a small thing but can make a huge difference

b. **Pause:** A pause can be a very powerful engagement technique during presentations. Pauses are fractional silences that you intentionally give during various strategic points of the presentation. Whenever you are not getting the right word, use a pause instead of using a filler. Start doing this consciously for the first few presentations. Rehearse your presentations, look at your recordings, replay it and make corrections. This process will help you to overcome using fillers during presentations. In the next chapter, we will explore various other types of pauses.

Chapter 16

Power of Pauses

1. **Sense Pause**

    The sense pause is roughly where a comma would be in writing, but it occurs about twice as often. It is more frequent than the comma because while writing, if your audience cannot understand something, they can re-read it. Since this isn't possible in speaking, you must allow time for your audience to process the information. This is a way of grouping words in small parcels so that the audience can keep up with what you are saying. This pause usually lasts from 1/2 to 1 second.

2. **Transition Pause**

    The transition pause is where a period would be in writing. It separates one thought from another. Many speakers are unaware that they are speaking in run-on sentences. Audiences are not able to process rapid speech as well as we think they can, especially if the content is unusual, emotional, poetic, dramatic, or new. This pause lasts between 1 and 2 seconds.

3. **Dramatic Pause**

    A dramatic pause is used to set up and spotlight what you will say next. For example, "Do you know what happened...?" Pause, pause, pause. This heightens tension in your narrative and gets the audience involved. You have to highlight a dramatic pause by following it with a statement that rewards your audience for following it along with you. A dramatic pause can last anywhere from 3 to 7 seconds.

4. **Reflective Pause**

    A reflective pause gives your audience time to reflect. Complex or unusual statements need to be followed by time for reflection. This type of pause says to your audience, "I want you to think about that," or "I've left a space for you to think..." A reflective pause can last from 3 to 7 seconds.

5. **Pause for Effect**

    A pause for effect is shorter, usually just 1 to 2 seconds. It creates the feeling that something is going to happen and lets words hang in the air so the audience can play with them in their minds.

    These last four are advanced uses of the pause that you can implement to finesse your public speaking.

6. **Spontaneity Pause**

    This pause creates a feeling of spontaneity. It is a technique that suggests you are thinking about your words as you are speaking and not simply reciting something you have said many times before. This will keep you and your audience members interested, even if you are actually very familiar with what you are saying.

7. **Pause to Relinquish Control**

    This is particularly useful in Q&A situations. When responding to a question, it is easy to begin rambling or repeating yourself and weakening your response. Nail your response to the question, and then pause to indicate you have finished speaking.

8. **Sensory Pause**

    Use this to support a description that appeals to the senses. For example, "A beautiful warm afternoon," pause... "Imagine it," pause... "Willows softly rustling in the breeze," pause... "Birds chirping in the trees," pause... "Sitting with a cold glass of lemonade in your hand," pause...

Create heightened feeling in your audience by pausing to allow their senses to take hold.

9. **Pause for Emphasis**

The enemy of the speaker is sameness. An audience will get bored if they feel you are saying the same thing over and over again, even if you are not. Use pauses to delineate your key points. Keep your presentation dynamic so your audience does not get lulled to sleep. Use pauses to change gears.

Chapter 17

Mapping the Two Key Concepts

In the previous chapters, we spoke about two key concepts. One was the TELL, TELL, TELL and another was the five magical elements. If you have to do a 'match the following', how will you match the following? Try making an effort.

• TELL(Open) • TELL(Body) • TELL (Close)	• Open with a high • Engage the audience • Tell a Story • Have a surprise element • Close with a message

It is obvious that the 'Open-TELL' will be matched to the 'Open with a high' and the 'Close-TELL' will be matched to the 'Close with a message'. Have you decided where the other three magical elements will be connected?

All the other three magical elements that is 'Engage the audience, tell a story and have a surprise element' can be mapped to the Open, Body, Close TELL's in a presentation. There are presenters who will beautifully handle the placements of these three elements depending upon the context and the audience in the presentation. In TED/TEDx talks, you will find speakers opening the talk with their personal stories and closing the story towards the end of the presentation. This holds good even for participant engagement and surprise elements too.

Chapter 18

Managing Presentation Nerves

During my workshops, the biggest presentation challenge that most participants like to overcome is nervousness. In my view, even the greatest presenters will be nervous during their most important presentation. But they are well able to manage their presentation nerves. In my view, you cannot overcome nervousness but you can definitely manage it well. I want to teach you some key techniques to manage nervousness that has helped more than 10,000 presenters.

a. **Don't start when you want to start:** Most of us are nervous during the initial 30–45 seconds of a presentation and then we get comfortable. There may be occasions where there was a previous speaker who just completed his talk and the audience is still processing that information in their minds. It is important to give them time to transition out. Since the opening is the most important part of any presentation, you have to do that well. Never be in a hurry to start the presentation. When you walk onto the stage (it could be a remote stage as well), don't start your presentation for the initial few seconds. Walk in, look at the audience, get comfortable, rewind the opening statements in your mind and give a gentle smile. These few seconds will help the audience unwind from their previous presentation and mentally transition to your topic. They will be watching you and will get curious as to when you will start the presentation. That is the time for you to open with a high. Never start your presentation when you want to start your presentation. Start when the audience wants you to start your presentation.

b. **Drink a few sips of water:** When you are nervous, you might feel dehydrated. The dehydration will affect your vocal cords and the modulation will not be effective. Hence it is recommended to take a few sips of water before or during a presentation. You would have seen some speakers carry a water bottle during their presentation. When they are at a loss for words, taking a pause and having few sips helps them regain their composure.

c. **Visualization:** I had an opportunity to listen to the legendary Indian cricket player, Javagal Srinath, speak. Srinath was from a place called Karnataka in India. He is one of the few highly respected fast bowlers of the country. During my corporate days at SAP, we had invited Srinath for a leadership talk. There he explained the importance of *visualization* which he said was crucial for a game's success. The one technique that all the cricket coaches insist that players use is the visualization technique. Srinath said that before he begins his run-up, he visualizes the entire scene – run-up, passing the stumps, delivering the ball, the ball pitching and turn towards the batsman. Having visualized it, when he bowls the ball, more than 90% of the time the ball will pitch exactly at the same place as visualized. Everything in life happens twice. Once in the mind and then in the real world. My favorite book 'The Magic' by Rhonda Byrne talks entirely about the power of visualization.

This technique is practiced by people who have attained great heights in their respective fields, be they sportsmen, movie stars, martial art experts, musicians, artists or presenters. I sincerely recommend that you practice visualization. Let me share with you how I practice this technique.

Before I go into a meeting or a conference to present, I do a five-minute visualization exercise. I sit in a place where there are few or no distractions. I visualize myself entering the room carrying my water bottle and my index cards. Now I am slowly raising my head to look at the audience and taking a conscious pause before I start. Taking a couple of deep breaths, I start my opening pitch. As part of my visualization, I also foresee challenges and interruptions that could derail my presentations and think about strategies to overcome those. In fact, I quickly fast forward the entire presentation structure (using mind map) during my visualization process.

This is a very, very powerful technique. You will not realize the benefits you can derive unless you try this technique in your next presentation.

d. **Script the opening:** We all feel nervous or experience those butterflies during the initial part of the presentation. It is important to open with a high, else we will miss the bus. Hence, a great presenter will never take a chance. Most presenters script their entire presentation and rehearse it multiple times. I recommend that you at least script the initial four to five statements of your presentation. Well begun is half done.

e. **Intentionality setting:** During the initial days of my training career, my only objective was to receive good feedback from the participants and I would do anything and everything to receive positive feedback. But this attitude did not last as I started experiencing huge setbacks including participants sharing unsatisfactory feedback on my programs. Every time I conducted a program, I was very nervous since I was only focused on the program outcome and participant reactions. When I met my mentor, he asked me one key question: "Why are you nervous?" For this question, I had the following answers:

I am nervous because–

.... I am not sure what the participants will think of me.

.... I am not sure whether I will be able to do a good job

.... I am not sure whether they will appreciate me or ridicule me

.... I am not sure whether I might be perceived as incapable

My mentor told me that in all the above statements, the 'I' quotient was very predominant. This means the intention of the presenter is inwardly focused. He is only bothered about others' perceptions of him and this causes stress and, in turn, nervousness. Instead, what should be the actual intention of the presenter? The actual intention of the presenter should be to give value to the audience or the participants. To become a great presenter, one has to change the focus from inward to outward. The presenter should move away from the thought of what others might think of him to the thought of how we can add value to each and every participant. This becomes the right intention.

Every time, before I start my presentation, I do a 30-second intentionality setting. I tell myself repeatedly that the presentation is not about me, it is all about them. When I started setting the right intentions through the intentionality setting process and focused outwards rather than inwards in terms of adding value, my presentations moved to a totally different plane. Positive feedback started pouring in with appreciation. Many programs started receiving standing ovations. This is a very key mindset change.

Practice, Practice, Practice:
You would have heard this many times. The question is how many times do we actually practice what we have heard. I would have conducted close to two hundred workshops on delivering high impactful presentations to various organizations and diverse groups of employees. Irrespective of that, if I didn't practice the day before the presentation, the workshop never made an impact although I knew the content in and out. I have tested such scenarios deliberately multiple times. On the contrary, if I practice presenting multiple times before the workshop, the workshop never failed to create an impact. It is the same logic between buffer memory and database in computer architecture. Fetching data is always much faster when it fetches from the buffer memory than from a database. Very similarly, when we practice a couple of times before our presentations, all the

information can be easily accessed and hence you will not stammer or use fillers during the presentations.

The best ways to practice are:

a. Use your mobile camera as a video recorder. Record your presentations and play them back. What you think you are presenting and what you have actually presented will be different and a camera can be a great introspection tool.

b. Practicing in front of the mirror is an age-old golden technique that should never be missed out on.

c. A virtual platform like Zoom, Microsoft Teams or WebEx has screen and video recording options. Record your trial presentation and play it back.

Chapter 19

Engagement vs Participation

I learned an important lesson from my mentor that Engagement and Participation are not the same. In a virtual program, participation can only be a means of engagement. You can still engage your audience without their participation. Participation is making the audience respond to your questions or actions. Means of participation can be asking them to raise hands, making them participate in roleplay, requesting them to acknowledge or contradict your viewpoints and involving them in group activities. When you watch a movie or a soccer match are you engaged? The answer is 'yes'. But, are you participating in the movie or soccer match? The answer is 'no'. This means you are engaged without participating in the event. In a remote presentation, you have to rely more on engagement and less on participation. Engaging the audience through storytelling, video learning, demonstration of ideas/products, sharing of interesting and new concepts along with voice modulation can make your presentations impactful.

Some of the techniques that you can use to engage people during **virtual presentations** are:

a. You can record a roleplay and play it back
b. Maintain eye contact with the camera. The remote audience will feel that they are looking at you. Don't look at your video on the screen.

c. Don't do too many check-ins. Have designated interaction points after every concept/message.

d. Use chatbox as an interactive medium. Don't overuse it

e. Make your stories and examples engaging – otherwise, participants will google other stuff while on mute

f. 20–30% of the participants will not be engaged during virtual presentations. Accept it.

g. You have to tune your mind to believe that you are presenting 1:1 to many, unlike a typical 1: many classroom approach

h. Pre-reads are very important for participants to get an idea about what will be presented. Send the pre-read before the presentation

i. Virtual audiences have a limited attention span. Hence, time the virtual presentation to be within 90 minutes

j. It is important as a virtual facilitator to be skilled in the relevant tools like Zoom, Microsoft Teams, WebEx and Google Meetup.

Chapter 20

Stage Walk

When you are presenting in large conferences, it is important to know how to utilize the stage well. Great presenters have a strong stage presence and one of the key factors for stage presence is to know how to occupy the stage. Presenters use the stage to deliver key messages by taking positions. Positions are key places (on stage) that are already pre-decided by the presenter.

If you have ever have watched a play, you would have seen actors delivering key dialogues at certain positions on the stage. Whenever they deliver key dialogues, they pause, take up one of these positions and deliver them. I have seen many presenters/speakers walk up and down and across the stage throughout their speech. I call this the 'caged tiger' walk. In a cage, a tiger walks from one point to another and back again without pause. A caged tiger position will cause disengagement with the audience. My point is, whenever you want to deliver a key point/message, take a position. Whenever you are transitioning from one point to another point or from one message to another message, that is the time to take a walk on stage. Subconsciously, the audience will start to understand when you are transitioning and when you are delivering an important message – based on your stage walk.

Eye contact: I witnessed an event where a world-renowned Spiritual Guru delivered a talk on how to develop resilience. The talk went on for three hours and was so insightful that every person who attended it found it of immense value. The media was interviewing a section of the audience on the impact of the event. Surprisingly, every person who was interviewed told the media the Guru maintained a one to one eye contact with them. The media was confused – how could one person maintain eye contact with all three hundred people in the room? The Guru gave a beautiful explanation elaborating on the technique.

Eye contact is not looking at the eyes. It is something more than that. Skimming over the participants at a glance is still not maintaining the right eye contact. The correct technique to maintain eye contact is to look into each person's eye for a minimum of 3–5 seconds. After this time period, the presenter moves on to the next pair of eyes. This continues until the presenter has covered every pair of eyes. Once this is complete, he repeats the process again. Having practiced this technique for a number of years now, I can easily find out who is engaged and who is not, during my presentations at any point in time.

Having listened to the Guru's explanation on the eye contact technique, the media grew even more confused. They told the Guru that this technique might work for a small group of people but would it work for a larger group? The Guru then revealed two other techniques and both there were my biggest learnings.

Sectioning technique: Sectioning technique is dividing the hall into different segments and maintaining eye contact with each segment. I have a large family portrait in my living room. Whichever direction I view this portrait from, I feel the subject's eyes are looking at me. Steve Jobs enters the big stage, logically separates the stages into many segments and takes a few seconds to deliver a key point before moving on to the next segment.

Feet follow the Eyes: Your feet should follow the eyes. When you practice positioning your feet in the direction of your eyes, the audience in that segment will feel that you are connecting with them. The best thing about this technique is that the presenter can stand still in one position and yet make the audience feel connected.

To summarize, three techniques can help:

a. Maintain 3–5 seconds of eye contact with every person
b. Divide the audience into sections and maintain eye contact with every section
c. Feet follows the eyes

Chapter 21

Curse of Knowledge

Let me explain this with a story. Once, there was an erudite priest who traveled across villages to share his wisdom with the people. Usually, his charioteer transported him in his chariot to the places where he would hold his discourses. One day, the priest was expected to go to a village 100 kilometers away, for a scholarly event where he had to address a group of 5,000 people. Since it was one of his biggest orations, the priest spent day and night preparing for it. After many hours of strenuous preparation, the priest began his journey with his charioteer. On the way, the priest noticed a sudden change in the weather. To his dismay, as he continued his journey, the weather worsened.

By the time he reached his destination, thunderstorms, torrential downpour, and flooding had wreaked havoc in the village. Given these adverse weather conditions, no one attended his discourse. The disappointed priest shared his despair with his charioteer: "I have prepared day and night for this discourse. Now, I am very disappointed to see that no one has come to listen to what I have prepared." He then turned to his charioteer and asked, "What would you do if you were in my position?" The confused charioteer replied, "You are more knowledgeable than me – so, with all due respect sir, I will not be able to say what I will do."

However, to console the priest, the charioteer decided to share an analogy. "Sir, I have 50 horses in my stable. To keep them all healthy, I have to feed them at least five times a day. But, quite often I run out of stock, so I have to go to the neighboring village to buy food. However, by the time I return, 49 of my horses will be out grazing in the field."

The priest, who was paying close attention to this analogy, asked his charioteer, "So, what do you do then? Do you return the food to the market or do you store it for another day?"

The charioteer replied, "Sir, despite the 49 others grazing outside, one of my horses is still inside the stable, waiting for the food to arrive. I don't want to disappoint that horse, so I will feed it the food that I have bought."

Before the charioteer could end the story, the priest was taken aback and said, "You have enlightened me, my friend. Even though no one else has come for my discourse, I still have you here. Come, I will share my wisdom with you."

The priest shared the lecture that he had prepared with his charioteer. After two and a half hours, the priest stopped and asked his charioteer, "What do you think of my oration? Are you enlightened, my friend?"

His charioteer, however, was still confused. He said, "Sir, you stopped me before I could end my analogy. Although I will give food to the only horse in my stable, I will not dump on that one horse all the food that I have bought to feed the rest of the horses. Because he can only take so much in at once."

The priest was pleasantly surprised. He realized that the poor charioteer didn't have enough knowledge to grasp all of what he had shared. He turned back to his charioteer and said, "You have taught me an important lesson today."

What the priest learned is applicable to all speakers. It is not about the quantity of information you give, but it is more about what information you give to them, that matters. In other words, don't share all that you know, but only deliver what your listener or stakeholder needs.

I have seen this happen with many technical presenters. Technical presentations can be boring even for technical audiences. Technical presenters tend to present all of what they know, a bias known as the 'Curse of Knowledge'.

The curse of knowledge is a cognitive bias that occurs when an individual, communicating with other individuals, unknowingly assumes that the others have the background to understand. This bias is also called by some authors the curse of expertise, although that term is also used to refer to various other phenomena. *(Source: Wikipedia)*

Presentation is not delivering all that you know. It is about delivering what they (stakeholders) want.

Chapter 22

Audience Analysis Audit (AAA)

The most important factor is understanding the audience and this is known as audience analysis. If you don't know your audience, you cannot pull off the presentation irrespective of your expertise on the topic. Many presenters work on the content of the presentation not knowing who is going to receive it. AAA should start as part of your preparation process and end before your practice sessions.

Let us do a small exercise. I request you to write your answers to these questions:

Why are they here: *My audience wants to see the new product I am launching and how they can benefit from it.*

What are they like: *They are customers who want to invest in a good product. They are straight forward and don't have too much time.*

How will they benefit: *Currently, they are losing a lot of orders since their existing product is not flexible, This product can bridge the gap.*

What do you want them to do: *I want them to at least give me a time slot where they can see a full demo. I want them to share feedback after they experience the trial version.*

What can go wrong: *They might not agree with the price. The time slot is too short for questions and answers.*

How might they resist: *They might say that they are already happy with their existing product and not looking for anything new. They might also not agree to test the trial version of the product.*

What is your call to action: *My call to action is to get time next week for a detailed demo.* Once you have done this exercise, your entire pitch will change and become and more meaningful.

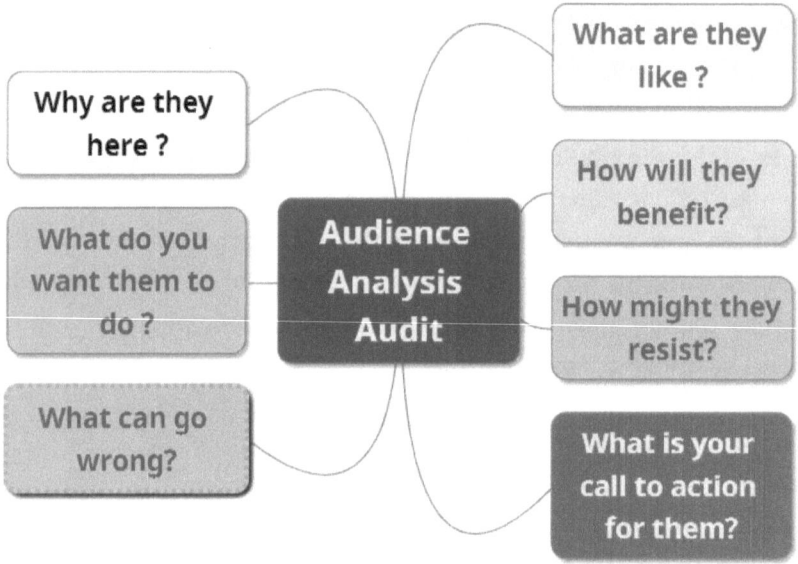

Chapter 23

Participation During Remote Presentations

When you are making remote presentations, it is especially important to have an explicit strategy to make the audience participate in the session. Although you cannot do frequent check-ins or expect acknowledgment, you can definitely have some planned interaction points to encourage participation. Here are some tips that you can use in your upcoming presentations:

a. **Polls:** Many virtual platforms offer polls. Polls are an extremely powerful way to get a quick pulse of the audience. Polls have to be designed and created in advance. Quite a few online platforms have a poll option. While triggering polls, I prefer to allow participants to mark their choices anonymously and the response has always been encouraging. The biggest advantage of using polls is that you can trigger participation in a few seconds and participants can immediately view the results of the poll. For platforms where polls are not supported, you could use an add-in called 'Mentimeter' (www.mentimeter.com). I love this extension because of the themes and layouts that this platform offers. It is a joy to conduct polls or quizzes through Mentimeter.

b. **Combination of tools:** Another strategy that has always worked for me is a combination of two tools. This becomes important because of the audience's lower attention span, specifically during remote presentations. For example, suppose I decide to use Zoom as one medium and Telegram/WhatsApp as the second medium. In the middle of the Zoom session, I will give them a quick read or a video to watch on WhatsApp/Telegram and will ask them to write one word describing their experience in the Zoom chatbox. This breaks the monotony for them from being passive listeners. Sometimes, along with Microsoft Teams, I use YouTube as a second tool. I will put a quick YouTube link in the chatbox and ask participants to view and comment on the learnings from the video. Innovation that can add meaningful value to participants should be your strategy. Similarly, think about one or more tools as a powerful combination. Finally, it is not about the powerful tool. It is all about the powerful use of the tool.

c. **Break Out rooms:** I love Zoom for their Break Out rooms. The Break Out room concept is helping Zoom surpass its competitors. Imagine you have 25 participants in the class and you want to split them into groups of five. This is possible through Break Out rooms. There is an option where you can randomly assign participants or choose specific participants for each Break Out room. This is great for any group work during presentations or strategy meetings where the facilitator has the option to go individually to each Break Out room, share expectations, give directions and clarify queries. This is a great way to take control and streamline participation.

d. **Roleplay:** I find role plays a great strategy to trigger participation. I divide the audience into groups and give small case scenarios. The expectation is that as a group they must discuss and create a roleplay of a case scenario in the live remote session. For example, let us consider a scenario where there is a crucial conversation with an employee who has decided to quit the organization. I will act as a Manager and request one of the participants to act as the employee and we will simulate a real-life situation through the virtual platform. Participation and engagement will definitely be high in this case.

e. **Chatbox:** Unlike in a classroom, you cannot ask participants to vocally answer your questions. In a virtual platform, you might have more than a hundred participants attending your webinar. In that case, the chatbox is the only tool for interaction. I usually have three or four planned interaction points in my 90-minute webinars wherein I request participants to give an explicit acknowledgment of their understanding of the topic, or any questions they may have on the contents I have covered. You can also direct them to record their free-flowing thoughts during the presentation in the chatbox.

f. **Whiteboard:** Whiteboard can be a great tool for a scribe during presentations. Many online presentation platforms come with their own whiteboard options including highlighter, text box, eraser and other features. I found Microsoft Whiteboard to be a great tool to give participants the experience of a real whiteboard. This tool also allows you to import images, pdf. and word documents for a seamless experience

Chapter 24

Hacking Any Tool for Online Presentations

There are many virtual platforms available for delivering presentations, like Zoom, Skype, Microsoft Teams, Air Media, WebEx and many others. Don't be intimidated by new tools. Although the mobile phone industry is maturing rapidly, irrespective of the model, we use a maximum of four to five features of the phone. Similarly, all we have to do is learn those four or five key features in any virtual platform.

The key features:

a. **Mute and Unmute All:** As a presenter, it is important to know the menu option and the shortcut key for the Mute and Unmute All options. It is important to mute the participants throughout the program and request them to unmute whenever they have queries or clarifications. While delivering a virtual presentation, you have to engage the participants all the time without any time delays, hence knowing and practicing the short cut keys to Mute and Unmute All becomes critical.

b. **Screen sharing:** This is another critical feature to be mastered. This option allows you to share the screen with others. You will be offered the option of sharing an application or sharing an entire screen. Please choose appropriately. When you choose to share the screen, make sure that all other windows which are not relevant to your presentation are closed.

c. **Video and Audio sharing:** If you share a screen, then the video will by default be visible to the participants. But you must take care to check that the audio enabling feature for streaming the audio across the audience is on.

d. **Chatbox:** There are special settings for the chatbox to be enabled based on the type of presentation. For large scale webinars, it is recommended you disable the audio function. Chatbox will be the only medium of interaction in such large events and can be powerfully used. You can also control the participants from asking questions in the middle of the presentation.

e. **Whiteboarding:** Most platforms offer a whiteboarding tool. Please make use of it. I prefer to have an external digital notebook for whiteboarding. This reduces my dependency on the platform.

Chapter 25

Sourcing Visual Images for Making a Beautiful Deck

It is important to take extra care in making your presentations aesthetically pleasing. For this, it is vital to source relevant images from the image banks. I would like to share with you some of the sources that I found useful for good quality images:

- **Prezi:**
  - Cloud-hosted application with a zooming interface
  - Zoom in and Zoom out for your presentation
  - Add multiple 3D backgrounds to images

- **Haiku Deck:**
  - Free online presentation tool
  - Helps to focus on key ideas
  - Millions of free images
  - Easy to use with drag & drop

- **Canva:**
  - Free online graphic design tool
  - Hundreds of presentation layouts
  - Auto resizing of text based on the message

- **Pixton:**
  - Beautiful comic characters can be inserted
  - These characters come in different costumes
  - Can be powerfully used for character narration

Chapter 26

Handling Difficult Audiences Tactfully

There will be always a few difficult members in every audience during your presentations. You cannot avoid them. You can only manage them.

    a. **The Deviator:** These are people who will deviate from the direction of your presentation knowingly or unknowingly. It is important to make a note of these people. You will find them asking unrelated questions and the presenter often gets side-tracked into answering all these questions and runs the risk of not being able to complete the presentation on time.

    Strategy: Use a parking lot technique. A parking lot is a place where you park all the questions which are not directly related to the topic that you are addressing. The presenter must inform the audience at the start of the presentation about the parking lot. So whenever you see a person asking questions unrelated to the topic, acknowledge the question and move it to the parking lot to be dealt with at the end of the presentation if time permits. Once you do this, others also will understand that they should only ask questions related to the topic.

    b. **The Challenger:** There will be a few challengers among your audience in every presentation. Some may be rude while some might be tactically smart. They will question the authenticity of the data, source, beliefs and sometimes, emotions too. Don't get thrown by these. Whenever I am presenting, I write down the top 10 questions that others may challenge me with and prepare to mitigate these before my event. If someone challenges me on the emotions (subjective), I give them a gentle smile and softly tell them that it is my personal point of view. If they challenge my data, I will make sure that I provide the right references.

Chapter 27

Making Numbers Meaningful

I have been to many corporate organizations to conduct various leadership and management workshops. Most of the time, I end up having lunch in those corporate offices. When I walk up to the food counter in the Cafeteria, I never fail to notice a board that often says: "Don't waste food." This message is clear, but not impactful. In a select few corporates, the representation of the message is even more impactful. The board near the food counter says. "For every plate of food that you waste, at least two people can be fed." This makes a much deeper impact.

The Akshaya Patra Foundation is an NGO in India implementing the Mid-Day Meal Scheme. It provides freshly cooked, nutritious mid-day meals in India to 18,00,907 children across 19,039 Government schools and Government-aided schools. This children's NGO serves locally palatable, wholesome meals from its 52 kitchens operating in 12 States and 2 Union Territories. Every time they raise funds, they give us data that talks about how many children were impacted by this foundation.

Numbers or data become significant only when they are made meaningful. Make numbers meaningful in your presentations. In one of his keynote speeches, Steve Jobs talked about iPhone sales reaching the figure of four million. Immediately after this statement, he qualified it by saying: "…four million means, 20,000 iPhones sold every day." When an audience listens to this statement, it is a 'wow' moment. Many of them might not be able to relate to four million, but we can easily relate to and understand the impact of 20,000 iPhone sales every day.

When you are presenting data, statistics, numbers to your stakeholders, explain what it means to the business and present them with a relatable example. Numbers alone cannot make an impact. The meaning behind numbers can make a greater impact

Chapter 28

The Outside-In vs Inside-Out Approach

I was very impressed with the Golden Circle concept which was part of Simon Sinek's TED talk. During my workshops, the majority of the presenters start with 'What', then follow up with 'How' and then with 'Why'. This is exactly why they remain average presenters.

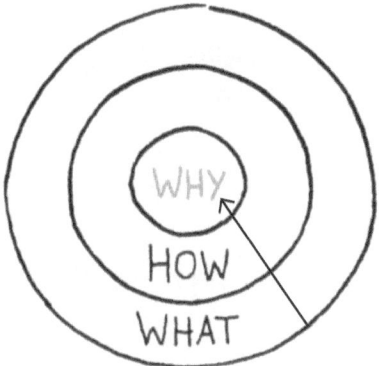

In short, this is how they present. This is called the outside-in approach.

Example 1:

a. What are the features of the product?

b. How it is going to be implemented/tested?

c. Why is the feature important?

Example 2:

a. What is the innovation about?
b. How this can be scaled up?
c. Why was this innovation required?

Simon says that the sequence should be entirely opposite. The great companies and great presenters start with 'Why-How-What'.

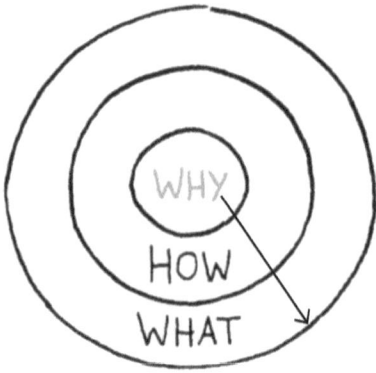

Sinek explains that 'Why' is probably the most important message that an individual can communicate as this is what inspires others to action. The neuroscience behind the Golden Circle theory is that humans respond best when messages communicate with those parts of their brain that control emotions, behavior and decision making.

This is how the great presenters present. This is known as the Inside-Out approach.

Example 1:

a. Why is the feature important?
b. How it is going to be implemented/tested?
c. What are the features of the product?

Example 2:

a. Why was this innovation required?
b. How this can be scaled up?
c. What is the innovation about?

This can be a powerful model to influence key decision-makers or stakeholders attending your upcoming presentations.

Chapter 29

The Habit Quadrant

To master a particular skill, you must go through a set of four stages – collectively called the quadrants of skill development or the habit quadrant. This logic is true for any skill. A person will have to move from the first stage to the fourth stage in order to co-opt any skill into his/her muscle memory. The quadrants are classified as unconscious incompetence, conscious incompetence, conscious competence and unconscious competence.

Unconscious Competence	Conscious Competence
Unconscious Incompetence	Conscious Incompetence

In the very first stage, unconscious incompetence, you don't know what you don't know. This happened to me in real life. After riding a bike for many years, I thought car driving would be a cakewalk. I cannot forget the first day of my driving class. Being overconfident, I told my instructor that I didn't require two weeks of classes. He patiently said: "Let's decide based on how you do today." This stage is known as 'Unconscious Incompetence' where a person doesn't know what he doesn't know.

He asked me to start the car and slowly release the clutch. I did exactly as instructed, but the car did not move. I tried again and again to no effect. After four attempts the car started and I changed gear. The car stalled at once. I repeated this similar iteration at least five times and then looked in frustration at my instructor. He gave me a gentle smile and asked me to try again. By now, I wanted to quit. I never thought car driving would be so difficult. This stage is called 'Conscious Incompetence' where you know what you don't know. This is the stage where a majority of people quit giving logical and illogical reasons. When you reach this stage, make sure you have patience and determination to move to the next stage, which is conscious competence.

The transition from conscious incompetence to conscious competence depends on your resilience and will to bounce back. In this stage, you will consciously start applying the skills that you've learned while being very cautious. You will know how to shift gears, how to move around in traffic and especially, to navigate on flyovers. Here the confidence level is neither too high nor too low.

Once you start driving more frequently, you will notice an abrupt change in your driving habits. You will unconsciously shift gears at the right time. This means you have shifted from conscious competence to unconscious competence, corresponding to the fourth and final quadrant which we call muscle memory or subconscious skill. This quadrant requires very low effort, but efficiency is extremely high. The only way one can reach this quadrant is after crossing all three quadrants. Unconscious competence is the stage of extreme skill development. Experiential learning is essential to reach this stage, hence it is aptly termed the 'habit quadrant'. It is akin to muscle memory that martial artists have – without even thinking of their actions, they act on reflex.

Once you reach this stage, you have essentially reached the pinnacle of skill development – to become an expert. In his book, 'Outliers', Malcolm Gladwell talks about his research on several successful people and how they practice a skill for at least 10,000 hours.

After reading the book, you might move to Q2. But, when you start applying the skills and techniques you will move from Q2 to Q3. My suggestion is to apply these techniques to your next six presentations or workshops. If you do that, you will transition from Q3 to Q4. I call this journey a joyous journey, where you will be able to make effortless, but impactful presentations.

Chapter 30

Learning Everything is Not Important. Learning What is Relevant is Most Important

Once upon a time, there was a Guru, who paid frequent visits to a nearby temple. His house was situated on the other side of the temple. Between his residence and the temple, there was a river. He usually took a boat to cross the river and reach the temple. Being an inquisitive person, the Guru often initiated conversations with the boatman.

One day, the Guru asked the boatman, "Hey friend, you have been a boatman for many years, you must have ferried people coming from different parts of the world. But, apart from rowing the boat, have you learned any other skills? Have you tried learning at least one other language apart from your mother tongue?"

The boatman hung his head in shame and said, "I am sorry to say sir, but I have not tried to learn any other language."

Guru taunted the boatman, "All these years of rowing passengers from diverse backgrounds, you haven't learned any other language? You have wasted one-fourth of your life, man!" The boatman kept silent.

Halfway through his journey, the Guru asked, "Let's put that aside… perhaps you are not comfortable talking to foreigners – but have you learned any other skill – like being able to predict the weather?"

The boatman was taken aback. He replied, "No sir, I haven't picked up that skill yet,"

The Guru sighed in disappointment, "You have spent the majority of your life in water, yet you have not learned enough to understand the dynamics of weather? What a shame! You have wasted two-fourths of your life." This time, the boatman kept his vision focused on making it to the temple and decided to avoid further conversation with the Guru.

With only a few miles left, the Guru returned once more to the topic of the boatman's skills. "I suppose even learned weather forecasters get the weather wrong, so how can you be expected to know? But still… do you at least know an art form like singing to keep the passengers entertained?"

The boatman wasn't happy and politely said, "No".

The Guru felt bad and said, "You have wasted three-fourths of your life, man… three-fourths!"

As they inched closer to the destination, the boatman noticed a leak in the hull which resulted in water gushing into the boat. To save himself, the boatman quickly dove into the water to swim towards the riverbank. However, he noticed that the Guru was still holding on to the sinking boat. The boatman shouted, "Please jump into the water and start swimming!"

The Guru in a bleak voice replied, "Sorry, I don't know how to swim."

The boatman smiled and said, "Sir, I am really ashamed of you. All these years you have traveled across the river, yet you didn't think of learning how to swim?! I have only wasted three-fourths of my life, but sir, you are going to waste your entire life because you didn't learn the skill that was most relevant to you!"

The key takeaway of this story is that it is not vital to learn any skill. But, it is vital to learn the skill most relevant to your current role. If your current role involves teaching a concept, convincing your stakeholder of an idea, selling a product, persuading someone to accept your views, then presentation skills are the most relevant skills that you should acquire. It is not just a skill that's nice to have, but a skill that's a must to have.

Chapter 31

The Last 'TELL' of the BOOK

Many technical and functional experts think presentation skills are in the category of 'nice to have'. Unfortunately, they miss out on a lot of opportunities unknowingly. When technical and functional skills are at an equal capacity for individuals, presentation skills can be a great differentiator. It is not enough to have an idea, but it is important to present the idea well to the appropriate audiences within the stipulated time. You may have watched the 'Shark Tank' series where many of the great ideas are rejected simply because they were not presented well. I am on the innovation and presentation panels of many organizations where we shortlist ideas for international summits. Many breakthrough ideas are rejected just because of poor presentation.

Like any other skill, anyone can master the skill of presentation with preparation and practice. I wanted to highlight some key pointers before you complete reading the book.

a. Do the AAA (Audience Analysis Audit) before any presentation (Chapter 22).
b. Always start preparing with the mind map (Chapter 12).
c. After this, support your message with a visual representation. This is where you make the slides (Chapter 13).

d. Build engagement into your presentations. Increase engagement and decrease participation in your virtual presentations (Chapter 19).

e. Maintain eye contact with the camera (for remote presentations) and practice it a couple of times. This is a very important technique to master.

f. Visualize the audience during practice sessions. Seasoned Radio Jockey's and News Anchors have mastered this skill and so can you.

g. Storytelling is a key skill. People of all age groups relate to stories and we are all good storytellers. Sharpen the art and science of storytelling (Chapter 9).

h. Fake it till you make it. If it is not natural, fake it initially until it becomes natural. Driving a car comes naturally to me now, after so many years. It takes time for any skill to become what we call 'natural'.

i. The future is going to be more and more digital and less face-to-face. Be prepared.

j. If you are planning on a long work career, don't ignore this important relevant skill.

About the Author

Author Rajanikanth is an industry renowned leadership expert with over 20 years of experience in consulting, coaching, facilitating managerial and leadership interventions to many leading corporates in the world. His clients include SAP Labs, Walmart, Adobe, Cisco, HPE, Visa, Qualcomm, Continental Automotive, Comcast and others. Rajani has impacted more than 20,000 people through his coaching and training interventions. He has conducted more than 300 workshops specifically on the topic '*Magical Presentations*' to various start-ups and leading multinationals bringing transformational results. The author has a strong project and people management background and was named as a top talent for many consecutive years during his decade-long stint at SAP Labs. Rajani is the CEO of WinnWin Leadership Academy (www.winnwin.org), a global leadership training and consulting firm.

Author e-mail: rajani@winnwin.org

References

https://www.fripp.com/the-importance-of-the-pause/

https://www.wikipedia.org/

www.TED.com

www.hbr.org

www.ingramcontent.com/pod-product-compliance
Lightning Source LLC
Chambersburg PA
CBHW030901180526
45163CB00004B/1659